Abundant Living

On Low Income

Eva Peck

© 2016 by Eva Peck

All rights reserved
Except for any fair dealing permitted under the Copyright Act, no part of this book may be reproduced by any means without prior permission of the author and publisher.

Graphic design and preparation for publishing: Eva Peck
Cover design: Eva Peck and Angie at Fiverr.com

Photography:
Pages 6, 42 and 72: Courtesy of FreeDigitalPhotos.net as follows:
Page 6: Photouten; David Castillo Dominici; Stuart Miles; Jscreationzs; Vectorolie
Page 42: Stuart Miles (3 photos); Ambro; David Castillo Dominici
Page 72: Stuart Miles (3 photos); Stockimages; Photostock

Cover photos: Alexander Peck (money image edited by Angie at Fiverr.com)
Author photo (p. 113): Jindrich (Henry) Degen

National Library of Australia Cataloguing-in-Publication entry

Creator: Peck, Eva, author.
Title: Abundant living on low income / Eva Peck.
ISBN: 9780992454975 (paperback)

Subjects: Finance, Personal.
           Quality of life.
           Success.

Dewey Number: 332.024

The book can be purchased online through:
www.pathway-publishing.org, Amazon and other outlets.

Dedicated to God, or the Source of All Things,
who has always supplied our needs;
and to our European parents,
who had shown us
how to live frugally and wisely,
and to later reap the blessings.

Other Books by the Same Author

Divine Reflections in Times and Seasons

Divine Reflections in Natural Phenomena

Divine Reflections in Living Things

Divine Insights from Human Life

Jesus' Gospel of God's Love

Co-author of:

Pathway to Life – Through the Holy Scriptures

Journey to the Divine within – Through Silence, Stillness and Simplicity

See also
www.pathway-publishing.org

Acknowledgments

First, I would like to thank God, the Source of All Things for enabling, inspiring and blessing this publication.

I must thank my husband, Alex, for his encouragement and support. He is always ready to help with editing and to give helpful advice. Without his valuable input, this book would not have come out as it has.

Finally, I would like to thank Justin Fraser, our financial advisor, for his sound-minded guidance over the years, enabling us to fulfil our dreams of full-time writing.

Contents

Preface 11

Introduction 3

SECTION I FINANCE PRINCIPLES 7

Chapter 1 Know Where Your Money Goes 9
    Expense and Income Analysis 9
    Creating a Balanced Budget 12
    Paying Yourself 14
    Financial Discipline 15
    Readiness for the Unexpected 16

Chapter 2 Minimize Your Debt 19
    Debt Avoidance 19
    Getting Out of Debt 22

Chapter 3 Make Your Money Stretch 26
    Conservation 26
    Maintenance 27
    Other Cost-Cutting Tips 29
    Careful Christmas Spending 32

Chapter 4 Invest Wisely 36
    Bank Deposits 36
    Stock Market 37
    Home Purchase 38
    Land and Other Investment Ideas 39

SECTION II SUCCESS PRINCIPLES 43

Chapter 5 Find Your Purpose and Set Goals 45

- Your Life's Purpose 45
- Goal Setting 47
- Daily Review 49
- Personal Example 50

Chapter 6 Watch Your Thinking 52

- Believing in Possibilities 52
- Transcending the Status Quo 53
- Avoiding Self-Sabotage 55
- Nurturing a Success Image 57

Chapter 7 Learn from Others 60

- Formal Education 61
- Self-Education 62
- Learning from Feedback 63

Chapter 8 Move Forward 66

- Personal Responsibility 66
- Controlling Fear 67
- Taking Action 68
- Help from Others 69
- Ongoing Quest for Improvement 70
- Relentless Perseverance 71

SECTION III SPIRITUAL PRINCIPLES 73

Chapter 9 Line Up with Higher Principles 75

- Experience of the Rich 75
- Andrew Carnegie and J. Paul Getty 77

    Benefits of Giving 79
    Important Keys.................................... 80

Chapter 10 Practice Gratitude.......................... 83
    Non-Material Blessings..................................... 83
    Matter of Perspective 84
    Health Benefits of Gratitude............................ 86
    Overall Improved Situations............................ 87
    Putting Gratitude to Work 88

Chapter 11 Possibility of a Higher Power......... 90
    Consider the Existence of a Higher Reality...... 90
    A Loving Helper 91

EPILOGUE.. 93

Chapter 12 Concluding Thoughts 94
    Different Concept of Success 95
    Narrow Uphill Path 96
    Purposeful Climb...97
    Help Alongside 98

APPENDICES.. 101

Appendix 1 Living on a Budget 102

Appendix 2 Income/Expense Analysis 104

Appendix 3 The Power of Thought 106

Appendix 4 Visualization and Affirmations ... 110

About the Author 113

About Pathway Publishing................................ 114

Preface

The purpose of this book is to help those who would like to free themselves from financial worries and improve the quality of their life.

"Abundant life" can be seen as far more than just material abundance, but rather include such intangibles as a purpose, sense of accomplishment, as well as happiness and contentment. Therefore, besides financial tips, the book also contains a section on success principles and a section on spiritual principles.

Written from the heart and in layman's language, the book is not intended to provide comprehensive information on the ins and outs of finances, success, or matters of the spirit. Rather, it gives common-sense principles based on personal experience gained over decades.

Specifically, it presents ideas on how to make our hard-earned money go further without sacrificing quality of life, how to sleep soundly without worrying about mounting debt, and how to live a more fulfilling life of accomplishment. It also brings out a few spiritual principles that can enrich life and make it more meaningful and abundant in terms of joy and happiness.

Most of these ideas and principles have been personally applied by the author and found working.

If put into practice, they can also help *you* to begin to free yourself from needless financial worries and raise your quality of life. Even if you have a low income, you can learn to enjoy abundant life. You may find that there is more than material abundance that gives our earthly existence meaning, joy and contentment. You may also discover wonderful and precious intangibles, which far exceed the satisfaction gained from physical possessions.

So let's begin the journey ...

Introduction

By way of introduction, let me share a true story. Robert and Yvonne have worked in various jobs, like most couples, since finishing their education in their twenties. They didn't have children, but Yvonne often worked only part-time. Living frugally, they saved money, which enabled them after several years to put down a deposit on a modest home. Apart from their home loan, they had no debts. With a fortuitous rise in the property market, their home evaluated, putting them in a good stead upon selling.

During their last five years of employment, in their fifties, they begun to feel that their jobs, while bringing food on the table, paying off a home loan, and even putting some savings in the bank, weren't entirely satisfying. They desired to devote their lives to writing where they knew that their talents lay. But how do you cover your living costs doing writing? Most writers don't. Only few become so popular that they can live on their royalties.

Eight years before Robert's eligibility for age pension, they felt that they had enough resources to stop work and pursue their dreams. Their house was paid and they had a moderate amount of savings.

At the advice of their financial adviser, they invested a significant part of their savings into the stock market and got into a scheme, which enabled them to receive a small regular income from their funds to cover their living costs, as well as receiving tax-free gains from the investments. Other income was very moderate and sporadic.

For over seven years, Robert and Yvonne had managed to live as a couple on less than what the government age pension is for *one person*. They survived a loss from the Global Financial Crisis of 2008 and absorbed the various inflationary price increases for goods and services. While many complain that pension payments are "not enough to live on but too much to die on", they had felt that all their needs were abundantly provided (since abundance involves more than money and things). They were happy doing what they enjoyed without lacking in any way.

Robert and Yvonne had not only been able to cover their food, utilities, property taxes, and insurance bills. In those seven years, they also acquired needed furnishings and appliances for their home; replaced several technological items (most things of that nature only work five years or less); installed roof-top solar panels for electricity generation; and finally bought a car (for seven years, they had creatively managed to live without a vehicle). Other financial outlays included several thousand dollars for extensive dental work, legal costs in a messy and drawn-out inheritance issue overseas, and miscellaneous house maintenance jobs that owning a property demands. They also finished additional study with the assistance of a generous government subsidy, created and have hosted several educational / inspirational websites as a public service; and self-published a number of books.

Robert and Yvonne are an average, not exceptionally gifted, couple. While blessed with good health, they had suffered two significant financial losses over the years, in addition to the GFC. Also, during their working years they had earned only moderate incomes. But following the examples of their parents, they have learned to stretch their resources.

In these challenging financial times when many are worried about keeping their jobs and paying mortgages and other debts, as well as covering their day-to-day living expenses, Robert and Yvonne chose to set their sights above the mundanities of daily life.

This book provides practical and proven tips on how you too can make ends meet on a small income and still abundantly enjoy life (where abundance is more than a lot of money and material possessions).

SECTION I
FINANCE PRINCIPLES

Chapters in this Section:
1. Know Where Your Money Goes
2. Minimize Your Debt
3. Make Your Money Stretch
4. Invest Wisely

Chapter 1
Know Where Your Money Goes

Many people are concerned about making ends meet. Money seems to run out while there are still some days before the next pay is due. This problem can be the result of not keeping track of one's spending and, as a result, overspending, where the outlay becomes more than the income. Things may be bought on impulse – perhaps they were on sale, but really were not needed.

When there is no spending plan, purchases can be made without considering what is really important to have money for – food, rent or mortgage, utility bills; and what isn't – for example, a meal at a fancy restaurant or an interesting household gadget that is on sale. Let's consider making a plan for spending so that there will be money for the necessities, as well as for some special things.

Expense and Income Analysis

Firstly, it is important to know where your money presently goes. To find out, do an analysis of all the money you have spent in a week, fortnight, or a month. To do this:

Know Where Your Money Goes

1. *Keep all receipts and make a note of costs where you received no receipt.*

   These are expenses for food, entertainment, fuel, and all other payments, large and small.

2. *Create a table on paper or computer where you have a column for the various expense categories.*

   Examples of categories are listed below, but can be adjusted to your specific needs by further subdividing, adding, or deleting.
   - Food (included can also be toiletries, stationary, postage, washing powder, and other regular household items)
   - Utilities (electricity, gas, phone, Internet, etc.)
   - Car costs (fuel, oil, servicing, insurance, registration)
   - Home maintenance (rent, repairs, insurance, furnishings, computer accessories)
   - Miscellaneous (this can be a catchall category for clothing, entertainment, books, and other occasional purchases)
   - Medical and dental costs

3. *Add up all the costs in the various categories and make a note of them in your table at the end of a pay period (week, fortnight or month, whichever applies).*

Some payments are made annually, some quarterly, others monthly, so if necessary, prorate these for your pay period. For example, if you pay $100 per month for electricity, the weekly cost would be about $25 and fortnightly about $50.

4. *Add up all the columns and work out the total expenditure.*

   Now you know how much money you have spent in a given time period. You can do this over several weeks to see what the average is. (See Appendix 2 for an example of finance tables for both income and expenses.)

Having analysed your expenses to have an idea where your money has been going, now analyse your income from all sources – job, pension, investments, bank interest, etc. Add these up and prorate, where necessary, for a month or fortnight, depending on how often you wish to budget for. For example, if your bank interest is paid quarterly, divide the amount by three to obtain a monthly gain. The total income from all sources over a period of time will become your usable income for that period.

Creating a Balanced Budget

The next task is to ensure that your spending is in line with what is available to spend, without getting into runaway debt. You might like to set your financial goals along the following lines:
- To have enough money for buying what is needed and a few extras for enjoyment.
- To consider every contemplated purchase in terms of whether it is really needed.
- To avoid unnecessary costs in interest charges.
- To have money left over from each pay to set aside for special needs and emergencies, or to save for something out of the ordinary like an overseas trip or an item of desire.

So let's see how we can create a balanced budget that will help us fulfil our financial goals.

You have analysed how you have been spending money and listed all your income. Now take another look at the expense table you have created. If your income and expenses are roughly the same, or better still, if your income exceeds your expenses, that's great – keep up what you are doing! If, however, your expenses exceed your income, you need to make some adjustments. To do that, consider what expenses in each category are essential, and cut out the rest. The essential expenses, with ideas how to reduce them, will include:

- *Food and basic household items* – you don't want to go hungry, but you may want to limit visiting fast food outlets. Instead, buy a few ingredients in the supermarket for healthier and cheaper dining.

- *Utilities* – these are essentials, but sometimes one can get the same service for less cost. You may like to check around whether you can find an electricity provider or Internet service provider that will give you a comparable service, but charge less.

- *Car costs* – a family car has almost become a necessity, with limited or time-consuming public transport being the only other option. However, if your family has two cars, could you get by with just one? Or, what about a smaller, more economical car instead of a four-wheel drive, that seems insatiable for fuel?

- *Home maintenance* – we all need a roof over our heads and a bed to sleep in. However, if necessary, costs can be cut by downsizing, reducing insurance payments by increasing the deductable or excess amount, and even possibly renting out a spare room to a student or a single person.

- *Miscellaneous* – this category may have several unnecessary expenses. Take a careful look at it.

- *Medical costs* – these will depend on each individual or family and their needs. Consider a healthier life style as a way to getting sick less frequently, and that way cut down medical costs.

Other ideas to keep spending within the limits of your income are:

- Question every expenditure. Even small amounts add up to quite a bit after a time.

- Learn from past spending mistakes. Have you bought things that now you wish you hadn't? Make sure that what you spend your money on is something you really need and will use.

- Whenever possible, look for sales. Also, consider buying used items. Often you can't tell the difference between second-hand and new items – and used things cost a lot less!

Paying Yourself

One more category needs to be added to your budget and that is *Savings*. We pay everyone else because we have to, but should ideally also include a payment to ourselves. This would be in the form of putting money aside for unforeseen needs or an emergency, as well as an unexpected opportunity or to be able to, in time, buy something special for our enjoyment.

Financial advisors suggest putting 10% of one's income in savings for this purpose. If that's too much, a smaller amount each period is better than nothing and will add up over time. To keep motivated to save, set goals and write down what you are saving for, for example, a trip, a new computer or a better car.

You'll reach your financial goals faster if you open a savings account at a bank. Money kept at home within easy access can soon disappear with the temptation to justify using it. Money that is banked is safe from impulse spending and also earns interest. Find a bank that best suits your needs – giving you a reasonable interest and charging minimally for servicing your account. Of course, don't get into a habit of making frequent withdrawals from your savings account.

Financial Discipline

The next step is to look again at both the income and the necessary expenses and to marry the two by assigning money to each of the above categories.

After you have made a spending plan that is within your means, determine to stick to it. This takes discipline and some self-denial, but is not impossible. In the long run, it will be worth the effort and sacrifice, and indeed rewarding.

If you avoid overspending and charging up your credit cards over what you are able to pay off when the monthly payment is due, you will save money on interest. Remember that banks charge around 20% a year interest on unpaid credit card balances. Money you had spent in the past may still be collecting interest, and you could be paying for things that no longer exist or are usable! These interest savings can then be put toward something special that you really desire as a reward for balanced spending and living within your means.

Readiness for the Unexpected

Having created a balanced budget and resolving to stay with it will go a long way. However, what if something unforeseen happens? In this time of economic uncertainty, this is not out of the realm of possibility. So let's have another look at your finances and help you to not only be covered when all is going well, but to also financially survive a major setback.

Consider the following:
- Are you on a cash basis (except for a home mortgage) or are your credit cards charged to the hilt? If the latter is the case, make a plan to get out of unnecessary debt, or consolidate your

debts, so that you'll pay less in interest. More on this later.

- Is your family budget dependent on an income that could disappear? For example, if one of two income earners loses their job, would it be a financial disaster? Consider living on one income and put the other one in savings. If you look hard, you'll probably find some unnecessary expenses that can be cut without a major sacrifice.

- How would you fare in case of an unexpected disaster – fire, medical crisis, or even death? Are you adequately covered by insurance? Where a young family is at home, some kind of income protection, disability insurance, and/or life insurance would be important in the event that the breadwinner became incapacitated. Also important is to have some savings to be able to draw on in emergency. In addition, make sure that you have made a will, so that in case of an untimely death, your grieving family wouldn't have unnecessary problems with inheritance issues.

In summary, analyse your expenses and compare them with your income. If you are spending more that receiving, cut your expenses to include only the necessities. Create a balanced budget and determine to stay with it. If at all possible, put some money into savings. This will help you to be prepared for the unexpected to which no one is immune.

For a succinct summary of the steps in this chapter, see Appendix 1. For an example of income and expenses analysis, see Appendix 2.

Chapter 2
Minimize Your Debt

Our parents and grandparents were brought up to believe that before buying large items, they would need to save to have the money. Newly-weds often started with little and built up gradually as they had saved money for what they wanted. General purpose credit cards were unknown till the second half of the 1900s.

By contrast, today one can live in luxury, but, on the flip-side, be head over heels in debt. The plastic card – issued not only by banks, but also individual stores – allows us to buy now and pay later, sometimes months, or even years later. By that time, however, the original cost has no small interest added to it. Paying off the original items – now possibly with considerable wear and tear – may become seemingly endless – and the mounting debt with high interest added can become a vicious circle.

Debt Avoidance

So, one of the key principles to make your money stretch is to, if at all possible, stay out of debt. This may be regarded as an old-fashioned, even obsolete, idea in a world where young people are not encouraged to wait and save for what they desire.

Neither is it fashionable to start small and upgrade when the money is there.

Western culture has acquired an insatiable hunger, almost greed, for material things in the hope that possessions will bring happiness. Ads lure us at every step of the way to buy now and pay later, or buy whether or not you need it and irrespective of if you can afford it. And the economy is structured so that it prospers when people spend – the more the better.

We are indeed powerfully and methodically influenced by "Hidden Persuaders" to borrow the title of a bestseller by Vance Packard, written over half-a-century ago, but still extremely relevant. Yet, to remain debt-free may still be the best way in the long run.

What can we do? Here are tips to consider in order to avoid being negatively influenced by the prevalent culture, to think for oneself, and to make wise decisions.

1. *Stop and ask the following questions for every contemplated purchase, large or small:*
   - Can I afford it?
   - Do I really need it – and will I use it over the longer term?
   - If the answer is yes to the first two questions, is it a good use of my money?
   - Is it likely to do for me what the advertiser promises?

2. *Realize that credit cards are good servants, but cruel masters – and so, use with caution.*

   I have found that one, or at the most two, credit card accounts is all that's needed. Having a credit card from every department store we visit unnecessarily complicates life. It also provides a temptation to overspend and lose track of where the money is going. Just ignore, or say no to, all the offers of credit cards that you may receive – even if they offer an incentive. In the long run, it is not worth it.

   Pay off the total credit card balance every month by the due date. This will help you keep track of how much you have spent and most importantly, there will be no extra cost for interest. Remember that the annual interest on credit cards is often around or close to 20% and is compounded on any unpaid balance, and therefore, the charges add up very quickly.

3. *Don't allow yourself to be pressured into buying.*

   As a principle, we almost never buy from door-to-door salespersons, no matter how good the deal sounds, or how persuasive the doorknocker is. I recommend you give yourself time to think about the facts presented – to sleep on it. If the salesperson says they can't be contacted later, or the deal is only available through them, I like to just politely thank them for coming, and then I forget about it. After all, I didn't ask for whatever they are offering, haven't missed it, and most likely can live without it. If I start seeing a need, I'll visit a store or search the Internet to make the best purchase then.

4. *Make a shopping list and stick to it in most cases.* Before doing your shopping, write down what you need. Resist the temptation to add to the cart items that are on sale, but that you don't really need. Ask the questions listed in point 1 above before making an exception to the shopping list rule.

Getting Out of Debt

Obviously, there are certain things one cannot buy without borrowing money. One of these is a home. If possible, home ownership with a bank loan may be more advantageous in the long run than renting. While paying off your home loan month after month for twenty, or even thirty, years, in the end you'll own the property, which will also most likely have risen in value. You will be better off than having paid rent for the same number of years and have nothing.

So a home loan is wise, but only under certain conditions. You need to have an initial deposit and be able to afford the repayments over the duration of the loan. Stretching yourself initially may be worth it. However, carefully consider the potential danger of not being able to make your payments if one of a couple loses their job, another baby arrives, or something unforeseen happens. If you default on mortgage payments, you could lose the property, as well as what you had already invested in it. Wisdom and prudence are called for in this type of long-term investment decision.

Here are other tips for getting out of debt:

1. *If you are in debt, other than paying off your mortgage, plan to minimize the debt as quickly as possible.*

    Small loans and credit card debt carry higher interest than home loans. Therefore check to see if you can consolidate your debts, such as house, car, furniture, etc. Ask about adding a little to your mortgage loan to pay off the smaller items. Then make slightly bigger monthly payments. This way you'll have just one loan to worry about and pay the lowest possible interest.

2. *Resolve to pay your credit card debt off as soon as possible.*

    At close to 20% interest per year, it is just costing you too much and you are gaining no benefit. Think of the money you could save if you had no interest to pay and what you could buy instead! Resolve to put aside each month a certain sum, the bigger the better, towards paying off the debt. Over a period of time, it will be encouraging to see the debt (and the interest paid on it) diminish. Plan to celebrate or reward yourself in some way when you achieve the goal of paying off your credit card debt. Then resolve to always pay the full balance by the due date so as not to accrue any further interest.

3. *Have the discipline not to add to your debt, unless it is totally unavoidable.*
See if you can cut other expenses as much as possible to live within your means. Downsize if necessary – be it selling a second car or exchanging the present family car for a smaller, more economical one. Could you manage without a car – even temporarily? It is worth considering – there can be some advantages other than cost saving. Could you make do with a smaller home in an area better connected by public transport? Look at your life style and your expenses and see if there is anything that can be cut.

4. *Increase your monthly loan repayment, or make payments every two weeks instead of once a month.*

This is another way to save on interest from your loan. It will not make much difference to your monthly budget, but will considerably shorten the life of your loan and the total interest paid. When taking out a loan, ensure that there is no pre-payment penalty – being charged for repaying the loan faster or in a shorter time than originally agreed. If there is such a stipulation, consider a different loan or another lending institution.

To sum up, never forget that credit is a good servant, but a cruel master. To keep it under control, evaluate each contemplated purchase, use credit cards cautiously, don't be pressured into buying anything, and plan your shopping with the help of a shopping list. If you are in a runaway debt situation, make a concerted effort to pay off your debts little by little through debt consolidation and paying your credit card monthly balance in full when it is due. Then determine to keep your debts under control, so that credit can serve you rather than oppress you.

Chapter 3
Make Your Money Stretch

One way to save is to try to make what you have last. I know that things are not made to work as long as they used to in previous generations, and that it often costs more to get something repaired than to replace it. However, there are still ways to make what we have last longer and as a result make our money go further.

Conservation

Firstly, don't waste resources – it will help the environment, as well as your pocket book. Here are some ideas:

1. *Reduce your utilities bill by conserving.* For example, switch off lights when you leave a room and aren't coming back for a while. Conserve water by having shorter showers. Adjust the thermostat by one or two degrees so that the air-conditioner or heater runs less. Over time, these simple measures will make a difference to your utilities bill.

2. *Downsize – and pay less for – services you don't need.*
Have a look at your Internet plan and phone plan,

for example, where there may be fixed charges for the data downloading amount or the number of calls. Don't pay for a large amount of downloading if you are only sending out a few emails per week.

3. *Evaluate subscriptions – be it online or by mail.*
Are you using all the services you have subscribed to – newspapers, magazines, books, CDs, online clubs? Subscriptions are often easy to get into – the initial offer of a free or near-free item may be hard to resist. Then the item, such as a newspaper or online information downloads come every day, week or month, but time or other factors get in the way of us using them. Payments may be automatically deducted from our bank or Paypal account without us even noticing. The key question is: Are you making a full use of the service? Unsubscribe from anything that is not necessary or useful to you.

Maintenance

Secondly, maintain what you have to make it last longer so that you will need to replace it less often. Some tips include:

1. *Take good care of things.*
Learn to do simple repair jobs, such as stitching up a broken seam on a piece of clothing or a small

hole in a sock, rather than quickly discarding the item and buying a new one.

2. *Keep things that are still functional for longer, rather than buying new ones every year or two.*
It is not necessary to have the latest model car, computer, or kitchen appliance – as much as the advertisers try to convince us to the contrary. If something malfunctions in a small way, see if you can get it fixed for less than the cost of a new appliance.

3. *Look after your health by eating a healthy diet, exercising, and getting sufficient rest.*
Kick any destructive habits, such as smoking or excessive drinking. You will save money in two ways – on the cigarettes or alcohol, as well as on potential doctor visits due to self-induced health problems. Instead of frequent eating at fast-food places, buy wholesome, nutritious, natural foods in the supermarket which are often much cheaper. Learn the art of simple food preparation – it doesn't have to be complicated or greatly time-consuming. Then save on medicines and doctor's bills, because you are likely to have fewer colds, headaches, flus, etc. Not only will you feel better, but your finances will also be healthier.

This will give you less stress – another health promoting measure.

Other Cost-Cutting Tips

By following several other principles, you can significantly reduce your living expenses. Let's start with the basics – food and shelter.

To stretch your *food budget*, consider:

1. *Making a shopping list and sticking to it.* Before going shopping, write down everything you need. A good way to build the list is to jot down items when you notice that they have almost run out. For example, when the flour bag or tomato sauce bottle is close to empty, write down the items on a shopping list. In the store, resist the temptation to add to the cart things not on the list – no matter whether or not they are on sale (unless of course you have unintentionally left them off the list and you really need them.)

2. *Shopping only once a week.*
   Plan your weekly menu and see if you can get everything in one shopping trip. Divide your monthly budget into roughly four parts and as much as possible, stay within your weekly allotment.

3. *Preferring larger supermarkets to smaller shops.*
   If on a tight budget, your money will go further in these stores as they tend to be lower priced. You also have more choice and can select cheaper products over more expensive ones, where the quality is not greatly different. Prefer home brands over other brands, as often you will pay more just for the brand name.

4. *Preparing your own meals as much as possible.*
   Rather than buying a lot of canned and processed foods, consider a bag of beans, peas or lentils. Each can be combined with a bit of meat and/or some vegetables and placed in a pot or slow cooker. With very little time and effort spent in the kitchen, they can make tasty, delicious and nourishing soups or stews. And best of all, the meals are healthy and inexpensive.

As far as your second basic need, *shelter*, consider:

1. *Downsizing, if your accommodation is unnecessarily big.*
   If there is only two of you, for example, consider a two-bedroom apartment or a small house. Of course, the cost of a move needs to be considered in the context of the overall expenses – but the move might pay for itself before too long.

2. *Sub-letting a room.*
   If the children have left the nest and you have a spare room, could a single person rent it to help with your rent or mortgage payments?

3. *Taking a look at the utilities.*
   Check to see if another supplier can provide you electricity, gas, water, phone and Internet services for a lower cost. There may be a number of competing companies providing these services. Shop around and check what each one offers.

4. *Repairs and insurance.*
   Again, if repairs become necessary, check around and get several quotes. You may be amazed how similar services vary in price. You can reduce insurance in two ways – by comparing quotes from different companies and by increasing the sum you would pay yourself before making a claim. Chances are good that nothing will happen, and by agreeing to a bigger deductable, your premium will decrease while you are still protected in case of a major problem.

Regarding other costs, such as clothing, appliances and entertainment, again, you can reduce these by shopping around. Often you can buy economically without sacrificing quality. Sometimes, even a second-hand reconditioned item can be a good low-cost purchase. You can always upgrade when finances become better and you don't have to be concerned about every dollar.

Checking around also applies to holiday travel – there are significant cost differences in airfares, hotel accommodations, and eating out. And if you are on a really tight budget, consider camping or simple day trips. Use your imagination and resourcefulness in coming up with ideas for enjoying life on a limited budget. There certainly are ways and means to do that.

Careful Christmas Spending

Christmas is a time when we like to do special things, including buying special foods and giving gifts. While these activities have their place, if one is on a tight budget, care needs to be taken not to overspend. If not careful, it is easy to get carried away by the spirit of the season and run up a credit card debt that we could still be paying off next December. The following tips might help in ensuring that both the Christmas season and the new year are financially happy times.

1. *Plan ahead.*

    Ideally, begin your planning in January. Make a reasonable Christmas budget, for example, 2% of your annual food and miscellaneous items budget. Then start your Christmas saving at the beginning of the year by putting aside a small sum each week. You will hardly notice this sum missing, but over the weeks and months, it will grow nicely.

2. *Evaluate your gift-giving list.*
   If budget is tight, talk to the family and consider options such as limiting gift buying only for the children in the family and/or just the immediate family – not the nephews, nieces, cousins, etc. Another way is for each person to pull a name out of a hat and buy gifts only for the person whose name has been drawn.

3. *Take advantage of sales.*
   By planning ahead, you can make use of sales and discounts that you encounter during the year – even post-Christmas sales! Sometimes you may find inexpensive things at yard / garage / rummage sales. People often sell unused items at a greatly reduced price and these can make lovely gifts.

4. *Be resourceful.*
   Consider creating a gift using your own talents. This may cost you very little in terms of money, yet be greatly appreciated, and even treasured.

For example, can you paint a picture, create a wood carving, sculpt a mug, knit a jumper, or make a quilt?

5. *Avoid impulse buying.*
   Don't wait till the last week before Christmas to buy gifts. With the pressure of the situation, it is easy to get frustrated, buy on impulse and without thinking, and overspend. Rather, accumulate your gifts progressively, or slowly and steadily work on creating gifts for others.

6. *Watch the credit card.*
   While the plastic card is convenient to use, keep track of how much you are charging on it. Don't charge more than you are able to pay off within the interest-free period. Or, if the temptation is too great, simply resolve not to use the credit card and only spend a predetermined cash amount. Once the cash is gone, your shopping is finished – even if you haven't got a gift for everyone you had in mind. Better that than waking up in January or February with a credit card hangover that will take you a better part of the year to pay off – with a high interest percentage added, of course.

By exercising discipline and responsibility in connection with Christmas, you can enjoy the season as well as the coming year – with no unnecessary financial headaches and setbacks.

To sum up, make your finances stretch by avoiding waste and looking after what you have. In addition, examine ways to make your food and shelter budget go further, shop around to get the best price for your other needs, and be careful not to overspend with Christmas shopping.

Chapter 4
Invest Wisely

It is prudent to invest in something that will bring back reasonable returns. Broadly speaking, there are two basic types of investments – real estate and the stock market. They can both work, but which is better will depend on each individual situation.

If you can, start saving and investing at a young age – even if your resources are small. With time and the development of your career, you will not miss the money that you have invested and it can grow into a nice nest egg that will come handy later in life.

Bank Deposits

If you have little money to invest, put at least a small, but regular sum aside each month into a bank account. Ten percent of your income is a good guideline that financial advisors tend to agree on – but if that is too much, any amount is better than nothing and will increase with regular deposits. The interest on a *savings account* may not be much – perhaps 2-3% – but it will grow and compound with time.

Apart from generating interest, the money will be there for you in case of an unexpected emergency. Also, over time you may have enough for a deposit to buy a home – which is almost always an excellent investment, as long as you can afford the mortgage payments. So start with a savings account and patiently watch your money grow over time.

If you know that you will not need a certain sum of money for several months, consider a *term deposit*. It pays more interest than a savings account and you can decide on the term, which can be anything from one month or less to one year or more. Three to four-month term seems the most popular and often the most advantageous as far as the interest amount paid.

When you put your money into a bank account, the money will be invested further – the bank will again put it in either the stock market or real estate. You may be able to receive more profit by avoiding the "middle man" – the bank – and investing directly.

Stock Market

Investing in the stock market broadly includes buying shares, managed funds, and precious metals (such as gold). For those who are not familiar with the system, this option can seem intimidating and a bit overwhelming – it was for us, until we learned more about it.

It can be good to work with a trustworthy financial advisor who can help you invest your money soundly and based on your situation and needs. While financial advisors don't work for free, a good one can be worth the fees they charge. You will have peace of mind and also the fees are subtracted from your investment gains, so in a way, you don't have to worry about them and are not directly aware of them.

Investments can be conservative with a moderate gain and low risk of loss, as well as more aggressive with potentially greater yields, but also greater losses. The degree of risk that one is willing to take for a potentially greater gain depends on each person and their situation.

Historically, the stock market has had short-term ups and downs, but over the long term, it has gone up. Every few years, favourable periods alternate with unfavourable ones. However, the market has so far always recovered from both smaller and greater setbacks – even the Great Depression of the 1930s and the Global Financial Crisis of 2008. So, the hope is that the market will again bounce back when the next downturn comes. And *in the long run*, the gain from your investment is greater than that from savings or term deposit interest. Also, if money is quickly needed, it can be gotten out of the stock market within a few days by selling some shares – which is not possible with a property investment.

Home Purchase

As far as real estate, investing in a home is a good step if at all possible. If you can save for a home deposit and qualify for a bank loan, this is an excellent investment with several advantages. The main one is that instead of paying rent every month, your mortgage payments go toward your own property. Most properties evaluate over time and when you finish paying your loan off, the home is likely be worth more than what you bought it for.

For this to happen, however, make sure that the location is as good as you can afford without taking undue risk that you won't be able to keep up the payments. Also, choose a home and location where you will feel good living for at least several years.

If you have to sell, for whatever reason, after only a short period, you may lose. This is because the costs of borrowing money, selling the property, and moving elsewhere may exceed the evaluation of the home over a short term.

So carefully consider the risk, and if it feels reasonable, seriously consider finding a home to buy. While debt is generally best avoided, a mortgage debt can be considered an exception to the rule if there is a relatively small risk of defaulting on payments and if the property is likely to evaluate.

Land and Other Investment Ideas

If you don't feel comfortable with the stock market – due to not having anything tangible in hand or for other reasons – and cannot afford a house or apartment, a block of land may be a good option. Again, the location will be important. If you keep the land over several years and it is in a good location, it is bound to evaluate. You can then sell it for a nice profit. Alternatively, as you have more money to put aside, you may be able to build on it. A brand-new house with a design of your choice can be a thrilling experience. And with the land paid, the home loan could be significantly less and thus easier to repay.

Even if you have no intention to build on the land, don't make the mistake we did and sell it prematurely. Let it sit, don't worry about paying property taxes and similar fees on it, and in a decade or more it can't help but be worth considerably more than what you paid for it. This is because land is a finite commodity and with increasing population needing housing, it will always go up in value.

Other, and smaller, types of investment can be something like solar roof panels or solar hot-water system that over time will pay for themselves by saving money on electricity. When paid off, they will actually generate a small profit – perhaps only $100 a month, but every little bit helps. The same can apply to roof insulation, which can save money on winter heating and summer cooling – besides being kind to the environment by saving resources.

So to sum up, wise investments (with the emphasis on *wise*) can help you get financially ahead. These can start with a small amount of regular savings or stock market investment. Real estate – a block of land, a flat or a house *in a good location* can be an excellent investment. The best way is to start regularly saving early in life and be patient. In due time, and without much effort, you will be rewarded.

SECTION II
SUCCESS PRINCIPLES

Chapters in this Section:
5. Find your Purpose and Set Goals
6. Watch Your Thinking
7. Learn from Others
8. Move Forward

Chapter 5
Find Your Purpose and Set Goals

Now that you are getting your finances under control and have less worry about making ends meet, you can give thought to other aspects of your life. What could make it more satisfying? Abundant life involves more than a lot of money in the bank or a lot of possessions. In fact the lives of many well-to-do, even famous, people show that while money can buy many things, it cannot buy happiness. This section touches on a few aspects of life which when brought into harmony with the laws of the universe will result in a satisfying life of contentment.

Your Life's Purpose

Leading life with purpose goes a long way. Discover what your purpose is – what did you come to the earth to accomplish during the few decades that you may have? This could seem like a daunting task, and might take time to truly understand. I believe that our purpose works on at least two levels. We all have a transcendent purpose, which I understand as being transformation by Divine Love into beings that are at-one with God. While the specifics of this are beyond the scope of this book, they are addressed in my book *Jesus' Gospel of God's Love*. However, we can start exploring our earthly purpose, which is easier to determine. Once we sense what our purpose here and now might be, life can become much more meaningful and enjoyable.

Often, an aspect of a person's purpose has to do with what they are good at and love to do. Look at your life – both past and present. What have you enjoyed doing? Where have you met success? What have you felt attracted to – sometimes contrary to the wishes and expectations of well-meaning others?

Was it a painting you did at school that drew the admiration of the teacher and classmates? Was it a piece of writing that won you a prize? Or, do you enjoy creating things with your hands – sewing, sculpture, metal work, wood carving? Or, are you interested in tinkering with the insides of things to see how they work? Or, do you enjoy public speaking and teaching, or perhaps entertaining others? Or, are you at your best in a sport discipline? Or, are you interested in spiritual things and ministering to others in their suffering? We have all been given unique gifts and abilities. When we use them, even just here and there as a hobby, we'll find an enjoyable addition to life. And if they are a part of your paid employment, you are blessed indeed.

If you are at the beginning or middle of your working career and your work is not quite in line with what you would really like to do, consider if you can turn your interests into a form of livelihood – perhaps even just on the side to start with. Can you sell your creations? Can you teach your skills? Perhaps you can offer a short weekend course at U3A (University of the Third Age) for seniors or at a summer camp for young people? Check what opportunities for sharing or contributing are available in your community, even on a volunteer basis. Sometimes volunteering can turn into a part-time, or eventually even a full-time, job.

Look at what occupies much of your time and if it is not already happening, resolve to make it as much as possible in line with your gifts and what you perceive to be your life's purpose. If a job change is needed, it may not be feasible straight away – especially if the income is essential. However, keep dreaming, seeking, and also set some goals for incorporating what you enjoy into your life.

Goal Setting

As mentioned, consider picking up a hobby to develop your talents, even if it is just an hour or two on the weekend to start with. Set a specific goal to spend time weekly or more often if you can and to create something using your given abilities.

Is there a group you could join or perhaps organize to bring others with the same interests together?

When several people work together, their creations can be displayed and even sold.

One success coach defines *goals* as "go out and love something" – in other words, the goals we set should be in line with what we enjoy doing. An influential teacher advised to "follow your bliss", or again, see how you can do more of what brings you joy. With time, you never know what doors may open as you keep your eyes open to opportunities where you can use your gifts and abilities.

Here are a few specific ideas regarding goal setting. See if you can convert your desires to use your talents into measurable goals. Our brain is a goal-seeking organism – the subconscious mind will work on any goal given to it to bring it about. Goals should be as specific as possible and have a time to be achieved by. They should be big enough to stretch us – to even give us a breakthrough.

Jack Canfield, one of the experts in the field of success, advises to write your goals down in detail and review them daily. Even better, create a goal notebook and illustrate each goal with pictures. Write the most important goal on a card and place it where you can see it frequently.

Three things tend to emerge during the goal setting process – considerations, fears, and roadblocks. The first two reflect our inside thoughts and feelings. Take time to analyse each of them and see if they are valid. If not, now that you are aware of them, they can be dealt with and reprogrammed. Roadblocks are external circumstances. Look at them as opportunities for overcoming and growth, and resolve that they will not hold you back.

Once your goals have been formulated and written down, set a time by which you'd like to accomplish each one. Even if you don't meet your target date, at least you are moving toward one – and you can always set a new one.

Daily Review

Stay positive, motivated and focused on your goals. Also, make it a habit to spend some time at the end of each day on acknowledging your successes, reviewing goals, visualizing future success, and making specific plans for the next day. During the night, the subconscious mind will process this input in a powerful way. That's why it is important to go to bed with positive, edifying thoughts.

Keeping a daily success journal is another tool for success motivation. Include five key events for each day under the following headings: Success (the event) – Reason (why successful) – Further Progress (what more can be done) – Next Action (specific plan).

Finally, visualize the next day the way you wish it to go. While you cannot control what the day will bring, see yourself performing at your best in whatever situation you encounter. Making this a daily habit will make a significant difference in your life.

Personal Example

Start working toward your goals with confidence, making adjustments as necessary along the way as you receive new insights – that is a part of the process. In a few months, or a year or two, you'll be able to look back and be encouraged by what you have accomplished.

I will finish with a personal story. As a young child, I used to write poems. I ended up with two notebooks of them and even had one published in a youth magazine. Later in high school, my essay on the 1968 Soviet-led invasion of Czechoslovakia (my country of birth) in response to the Dubcek reforms got a special mention, being among the best three. That was a great accomplishment since I had then lived in Australia for just over a year and was still working on mastering English as a foreign language.

Later, in my working career, I was commended as a writer and editor of reports, procedural manuals, and various office documentation, as well as articles of spiritual nature. Later still, I returned to teaching, and found that creating lesson plans and student workbooks came to me much easier and was more enjoyable than the actual classroom teaching. From my writing during my teaching years actually came several academic books for students of English (co-authored with my husband).

On the side, as time allowed, I pursued writing on subjects of personal interest. I had hoped that one day I could publish my writings. Upon retiring from teaching now several years ago, I have been able to devote most of my time to writing and publishing – in the form of books and websites (see www.pathway-publishing.org). Even though the income from it is minimal, that is not of ultimate importance, as all our needs have been met. It is satisfying to see my writing in print, e-books or online, and know that others are being helped and edified.

Summing up, look at your life to see what you may be intended to accomplish while on earth. One aspect of our purpose is to use the gifts and talents we have been given to serve others. Once you know what your gifts are, take another look at your situation and set goals that are specific, realistic (though also stretching you), and to be reached by a target date. Keep these in mind, visualize the outcome, and move forward. Reward yourself when you have reached a goal and set a new one.

Chapter 6
Watch Your Thinking

Our thinking and expectations are powerful determiners of our success or otherwise. If you say and believe that you can succeed, you will be right. If you say that you cannot succeed, you will also be right. This is a sobering reality. Below are some tips on helping you succeed in fulfilling what you believe to be your life's purpose and calling.

Believing in Possibilities

Now that you better understand at least some aspects of your life's purpose by looking at what you are good at and what you enjoy doing, start incorporating this into your life step by step – if it is not already happening. Diligently look for ways and possibilities to use your gifts.

If your paid job is enjoyable and fulfilling for you – wonderful. You are already on the right track and have much to be grateful for. If it is not as much in line with your gifts and talents as you would like it to be, still be grateful that you have a job and an income, but consider ways of making your work more satisfying. It may seem impossible at first, but keep thinking, exploring, and talking to people.

Could some changes be made within the job itself? Can you make it more creative for yourself? Is there another department in the same company where your talents could be better used? You never know what doors may open at the right time – so keep looking and knocking, while remaining thankful for what you have.

Even if you don't see a way to get paid for what you like doing, explore ways how to use and develop your gifts and talents on the side. Then, if a door does open, you will be ready to walk through it.

Set aside time for using your talent. For example, make it a hobby; take a class to get better; teach your skills to your children or others; create things to sell or donate to a fund-raising rummage sale. Pursue your heart's desires to incorporate using your gifts into your life as much as possible. Visualize your dreams materializing and believe that it is possible. With time and persistence, this will happen.

Transcending the Status Quo

Don't follow the crowd – decide to be unique. Some find themselves in circumstances of a crushing debt and/or a soul-destroying job situation. If one or both apply to you, resolve to transcend the condition. We have already discussed the former – getting out of debt. Regarding the latter, again start with small steps and be patient. Sometimes a change of perspective can go a long way. Instead of focusing on the negative aspects of your job and feeling bad, look for what is good about it and be grateful. Gratitude is a powerful antidote to negativity and dissatisfaction.

Set achievable goals in the area of your talents and work towards them. Celebrate and reward yourself in some way when you have reached a goal and then set a new, higher goal. Believe in yourself and expect to succeed. Develop a can-do attitude rather than focusing on what you can't do.

If you are able to, share your goals and ideas with people who will encourage you. It helps to have a mentor or another person who believes in you. By the same token, be careful with chronically negative people who are likely to crush your fragile dreams before they have a chance to get off the ground. Sometimes well-meaning people can make remarks such as "that will never work", "be real", "you must be realistic", etc. Carefully consider all input, even the cautioning kind, and take from it what is valid. You are ultimately responsible for your decisions, so move ahead if after considering all the factors you still feel you should.

Remember that many people have succeeded in following their dream against great, almost impossible, odds. While your situation may be different, you can let such individuals inspire you to believe that you too can succeed if you are willing and able to pay the price it takes in time, effort, perseverance, and whatever else might be required. Step out, take a risk that you can live with, and see yourself as succeeding – even if it might take much time and patience.

Even if you don't become rich and famous (remember that most of us don't – though you might!), at least you'll have the joy of having your life aligned with your talents and gifts. You will make a difference in your own sphere of influence – and we all have one. And the satisfaction from serving where you can by using your abilities can be worth far more than fame and money. So even if your income remains small, there is no reason you cannot feel like your life is rich and abundant.

Avoiding Self-Sabotage

Many of us can sabotage achieving our desires by our own thoughts – often unknowingly and subconsciously. Mindfulness, or being aware of and able to observe our thought processes, goes a long way to realize what is happening. Once we understand the process, we can change.

Try to notice your thoughts and feelings as they arise – picture yourself as an observer of them. Stop and analyse the thoughts you observe. Are they negative, casting doubts that you can achieve your goals? Or, are they affirmative?

Remember, whether you think you can succeed, or whether you think you cannot succeed, you will be correct. Our thoughts are powerful – they in fact are energy – and will determine our future. They can even make us healthy or sick. The good news is, however, that once we become aware of our thoughts, we can change them. It is possible to see a situation differently – from a new perspective.

Visualize success for yourself. In your mind's eye, see yourself as doing what you love and succeeding. Hold onto this vision – even create reminders of where you are going in the form of post-it notes, cards, or pictures. Attach one to your computer, place another in your wallet, or keep them in drawers to see often. If you live by yourself, you can also stick them on the bathroom mirror, fridge, and wherever else you pass often in your home.

Of course, life can take unexpected twists and turns, such as accidents or debilitating illness that may prevent one reaching a goal. However, live in the present and focus on achieving your vision while you have the strength and energy to do so. Remember that success doesn't have to mean great financial or material abundance. The satisfaction of doing what you enjoy where you have just enough money to make ends meet can outweigh a well-paid, but less fulfilling job situation, especially when considered longer-term.

Another aspect of our thinking process is the critical voice inside. Its purpose is to protect us from harm. However, sometimes it becomes over-protective, perhaps still responding to a childhood incident, which at that time seemed traumatic. Placed into proper perspective and into the present, a fear of another trauma is no longer justified.

Realizing from what childhood experiences our subconscious fears, even phobias, come can go a long way towards consciously counteracting them and moving forward rather than irrationally holding back. One helpful technique to align the body energies and neutralize or release irrational beliefs lodged in our subconscious since childhood is EFT (Emotional Freedom Technique, aka Tapping). It is beyond the scope of this book to discuss in details, but a lot of information is available on the Internet.

Nurturing a Success Image

Most people remember and focus on their failures rather than their successes. That's because from our childhood, successes have usually been taken for granted, whereas failures were made a big deal of. Remembering our successes helps us to build a healthy self-esteem.

Make an inventory of all your successes. Start with nine major successes – three in each third of your life to the present. Continue the exercise and list 100 successes. These can include passing each grade at school, getting a driver's license, getting married, getting a job, etc.

Another good practice is to create a victory log – this can be added to daily and include such things as achievements, keeping personal disciplines, resisting temptations, responding to others in love, etc. Appreciate yourself for the various small and larger successes.

Also display your success symbols in your home or work place – prizes, pictures, trophies, diplomas, etc. to remind yourself of your achievements. Our environment impacts our moods, attitudes and behaviour, and your success symbols will subtly, subconsciously program you to seeing yourself as a winner, build confidence, and motivate you to further successes.

See Appendix 3 for insightful quotes on the power of thought, and Appendix 4 for tips on affirmations and visualization.

To sum up, our thoughts and our subconscious have a powerful influence on how we view ourselves and the world around us. They can promote or sabotage our success – both financial and in other areas. The good news is that we can, to a considerable degree, learn to control our thoughts and even reprogram our subconscious to avoid self-sabotage to fulfilment and happiness. Consciously resolve to act as though everyone is on your side and wants to help you accomplish your goals. See every negative event as containing seeds of an equal or greater benefit. Remind yourself of past accomplishments and successes. Then look for opportunities and see how you can use every experience to your advantage. If something doesn't go the way you had hoped, see it as God, life, or the Universe, having something better in store and expect this to unfold in due time.

Chapter 7
Learn from Others

As humans, we are a lot better off if we work together and cooperate with each other, rather than when we compete and strive against one another. In today's sophisticated and complex world, no one is able to remain on their own and hope to make sound decisions without consulting other people or sources of information. So if you are considering a life change or career change to eventually be able to do what you really enjoy, or even if you want to make the most out of your present situation, get as informed as you can. Learning from others may help you maximize your opportunities as well as avoid making unnecessary mistakes.

No one can be an expert in all things, and we all need to learn from each other and help one another grow and become better at what we do. Willingness to learn from others involves humility through the realization that we don't by ourselves have all that we need to fulfil our potential, and that we are all gifted in different ways for the purpose of complementing and helping others.

Some of us prefer classes and courses; others are self-learners from teach-yourself books or the Internet. So whatever your learning style and preferences, consider developing your talents and improving your skills by finding a course or other resources that can help you reach a higher level in your sphere of endeavour.

Formal Education

It is well known that knowledge is power. Education will help us get ahead. Those with higher education or training and skill in a trade tend to do better in life than those who only finished high school. A degree, diploma or a certificate are usually necessary to get a good job in the relevant field.

The educational opportunities nowadays are incredible and don't have to cost a fortune. Gone are the days when the only way to get a degree was to take out a big loan and to spend several years in university or college classes.

Online education has mushroomed in recent years. You can get a degree that way and may not even have to leave your home or pay much. So whether you are interested in longer-term study (a degree course) or just a short course for a certificate or a diploma, you should be able to find what fits your needs.

Often, part-time study opportunities are available, so that you can both work and study. If money is a concern, it may also be possible to apply for some kind of a financial assistance. One example of short-term free online courses offered by various reputable universities is *https://www.coursera.org/*. Explore the website and see if you can find anything of interest.

Self-Education

If for various reasons you haven't had the opportunity for a formal academic education, all is not lost. Many have acquired knowledge or qualifications later in life, or developed their skills to a high degree, which also is a form of education.

Depending on what you want to do, libraries most likely have books on the subject. Read widely and consider a range of views – then decide what speaks to you and put it into practice.

Consider self-help books to develop yourself. Take a personal inventory and look for books about personality development and human relationships. There are also tests to see where your innate aptitudes lie and therefore what direction to pursue in life for maximum satisfaction and fulfilment. Regarding success principles, Jack Canfield and many others have written excellent books on the subject.

The Internet is an almost inexhaustible source of information – sometimes to the point of being overwhelming. And talking to successful people in your field of interest, if you have the opportunity, or reading their books can also be very helpful. Perhaps you can even get a mentor.

And of course, it is still true that practice makes perfect. So use your skills as much as you can, and keep looking for better ways to accomplish your short-term and longer-term goals.

Learning from Feedback

Being social beings, we all receive feedback from others – directly or indirectly, and whether we have asked for it or not. Feedback can be both positive and negative. Listen carefully and take a note of both.

While we don't generally like criticism and correction, it can help us stay on course to our goal if we are straying off course, or it can save us grief later. Therefore, avoid the sometimes almost automatic response to negative feedback such as ignoring it, getting upset with the person who gave it, or, on the opposite extreme, caving in and quitting. Rather evaluate all feedback on its merit. Is it sound or not? Are there facts the other person is unaware of? Does the feedback warrant acting on? Would it be wise to seek other counsel and get more facts? It is always a good idea to get as much information as we can on any pursuit or issue – to seek multiple informed opinions and then making a decision.

Feedback can come from without – circumstances, comments from others – as well as from within –

body sensations, feelings, hunches and intuition. Take note of red flags and yellow alerts, and never go against what doesn't feel right. Notice feedback patterns – if several people are hinting at the same thing, there is probably truth in it. It is better to be successful as a result of acting on unpleasant feedback than insisting on being right at all costs and then failing to reach our goals.

If you have failed in a certain undertaking, the following steps can be an appropriate response enabling you to more forward:

- Acknowledge that you did the best you could under the circumstances at the time.
- Write down all the lessons you have learned from the experience.
- If others were involved, ask what they learned to avoid making the same mistakes next time.
- If need be, apologize and clear the air of any misunderstandings or hurt feelings.
- Take time to review your past successes to regain confidence that you can succeed again.
- Regroup, refocus your vision, and move forward to realize your dreams.

In summary, using the means at your disposal, get as knowledgeable and proficient as you can in your field of interest. This will give you a better chance to ultimately reach a point, where what you believe to be your life's purpose, what you enjoy doing and are good at, can become your main endeavour in life.

Chapter 8
Move Forward

Now that you have determined where your gifts lie and how you can make a contribution using them, set some goals, and acquired sufficient information, make sure you are aware of the cost of success and willing to pay the price.

The road to success is paved with discipline, continued education, much hard work, and ongoing practice to reach expertise. It passes through tunnels of determination, doing what it takes, and putting in the necessary time.

It is important to first ascertain what the price is to reach a specific goal and then decide if it is worth the sacrifice. If you have counted the cost and are comfortable with it, it is time to move ahead step by step. This chapter gives a few helpful principles adapted from Jack Canfield's book, *The Success Principles*.

Personal Responsibility

We cannot control what happens to us – events or circumstances caused by various external factors. However, we can control how we respond to those events or circumstances. As we grow in awareness of our thoughts and reactions, we can learn to change them. We have a choice whether or not to get angry about something, whether to regard a situation as hopeless or see positive possibilities in it, whether to mindlessly react or mindfully respond.

There are three things we can control to at least some a degree, even if not perfectly: thoughts, mental images, and behaviour. Behaviour needs to change from habitual to intentional if we want different results in our life. Wise actions need to be taken and gut-level warning signals heeded.

Evaluate your life, determine what you want and what not, search for the causes of undesirable outcomes, and then focus your behaviour on what works and brings the desirable results.

Controlling Fear

Fear is natural, and courage is not the absence of fear, but acting in spite of feeling fearful. If we aren't willing to do this, fear may stop us from achieving what we desire.

Fear can often be the result of imagining bad outcomes – *Fantasized Experiences Appearing Real*. We scare ourselves by imagining that people will reject us, say no to our requests, and any number of other negative or even disastrous scenarios. Thus we create our own fear and thereby hold ourselves back. (There is of course a healthy fear that protects us from danger. Therefore evaluate whether your fear is in that category or mainly imaginary.)

One way to get rid of irrational fear is to replace the imagined scary outcomes with positive ones – imagine that things will turn out well. If a big step with a significant risk is too scary, start in small steps. This will decrease the risk and enable you to proceed step by step with the increased confidence of small successes.

Sometimes a "leap of faith" may lead to a real breakthrough. However, don't risk more than you can comfortably live with. Some people have a higher risk tolerance than others. The balance is to be willing to step out of your comfort zone, but only so far as you would be able to survive and recover from if things went wrong.

Taking appropriate risks and chances, having high intention and low attachment, and just pushing forward to the desired goal, you will eventually get there – even if it takes longer than planned.

Taking Action

Step out and act when you feel ready. Depending on the situation, there may never be the perfect time or circumstances, but sometimes it is better to be patient and wait. Try to discern this and move ahead when you feel the time is right for you. Make sure you have enough information, but also realize that you'll be learning as you go when unforeseen factors emerge.

Failure along the way is likely to occur as a stepping stone on the way to a higher plane, so don't be discouraged by it and quit. Remember that many a great achiever had failed numerous times before finally succeeding in reaching their goal. Acting with energy and determination – even without guarantee of success – creates momentum. Previously unseen help or resources may suddenly appear.

Don't wait to see the whole path ahead of you – take one step at a time and make decisions along the way as things unfold. Little by little, progress will be made to your dream or *even somewhere better*. Continue to explore, doing what you can, and eventually a turning point will come.

Help from Others

Many people are afraid to ask questions or request help because they fear rejection or being thought of as dumb. However, in reality, rejection is a myth – you haven't lost anything by being rejected, but there is a great potential for gain if your request is granted. An answer to your "dumb" question can save you a lot of heartache, and other kinds of help may propel you forward towards your goal.

Therefore ask regardless of what people may think of you and have a positive expectation. Assume you can get what you are asking for. Ask the right person – find out who is able or authorized to give you what you need. Be clear and specific about what you are after. Ask repeatedly – if the answer is initially no, with persistence it may eventually become yes. Ask a different person – perhaps a whole number of them. Persevere and eventually someone will say yes.

You have nothing to lose and everything to gain by asking. Many famous and highly successful people only had a breakthrough after going through dozens, even hundreds of rejections. Never give up!

Ongoing Quest for Improvement

Always strive to improve in everything you do. Set specific goals for improvement, realize that it takes time and effort, and improve in small increments. Practice, practice, practice – not skipping any steps. Sometimes the margin between the great and the average is relatively small, but significant.

Keeping a record of successes helps us stay on track and motivates us to greater heights. We focus on what we want rather than on what we don't want. Set a target in all areas of life and keep score. This will help manifest you vision and achieve your goal.

At the beginning of any venture there may be the awkward stage of "doing things badly". This is a normal part of learning. With time, practice and experience, you will reach proficiency and finally excellence. With the momentum built, benefits will follow for the rest of your life.

Relentless Perseverance

Practice persistence. High achievers refuse to give up despite obstacles and difficulties. They always get up after having fallen, never lose sight of their hopes and dreams, and try again and again till their goal is realized. For every obstacle, stop to think of strategies to get around, over or through the block. Always be solution-oriented and eventually a way will be found that works. Remember that when one door closes, another one is likely to open. Be on a lookout for this new door and ready to walk through it.

In summary, having counted the cost to reach a goal, take personal responsibility for your thoughts and reactions, evaluate the risks and control your fears, take step-by-step action, involve and seek help from others, always strive for improvement, and persevere, no matter what obstacles come up. By following these principles you can't help but eventually succeed. And even if your successes do not quickly bring financial abundance – this may take time – the satisfaction of achieving your goals and accomplishing good things of and by itself will make your life more abundant.

SECTION III
SPIRITUAL PRINCIPLES

Chapters in this Section:
9. Line Up with Higher Principles
10. Practice Gratitude
11. Possibility of a Higher Power

Chapter 9
Line Up with Higher Principles

Many people desire and strive for wealth and success, believing that a big income, large house, fancy car, luxury boat – for everything the bigger the better – will bring them happiness. If only they could afford a Mercedes or a Ferrari, or have a lavish home on a posh side of town, or go on an exotic holiday! But is this where true happiness is really found? Consider these real-life stories and results of studies.

Experience of the Rich

Carl had a very successful career as a consultant. Even as a young man, he travelled the world and made a lot of money. He and his wife had a beautiful home and a very comfortable lifestyle. In the eyes of many, they were blessed.

Out of over 5,000 applicants, Doug was one of only 80 selected to become an apprentice with a prominent bank. Within just a few years, he was repeatedly promoted, eventually being made the head of a major department at another bank. By the time he left that job to start his own company, he was making more money in one year than most people make in a lifetime. He too felt blessed.

Yet, both of these men are convinced that there are blessings that surpass material riches. For instance, today Carl volunteers as a teacher of spiritual principles helping others get closer to God. He remarks, "I have personally seen and experienced that material wealth does not lead to happiness. The struggle to get it and keep it allows time for little else. On the other hand, living by higher principles opens up so many blessings, such as a happy marriage, peace of mind, and a good conscience."

Doug similarly observes: "God does not want us to live a life of opulence. I strongly feel that whatever He gives us that is beyond our daily needs puts us under obligation to use it according to His will." Recently, he and his family started to learn another language in order to teach more people about God. He says, "We have learned that *giving makes us happier than does receiving.*"

Carl and Doug have both learned that spiritual blessings are much more valuable than material riches. And studies have now conclusively shown that giving is indeed a path to well-being and happiness – as shown later in this chapter.

Daniel Gilbert, a Harvard professor of psychology and author of award-winning, best-selling, and internationally translated classic, *Stumbling on Happiness,* notes that mental-health experts who have studied the relationship between wealth and happiness have found that wealth increases human happiness when it lifts people out of abject poverty and into the middle class. However, it does little to increase happiness thereafter.

"Once above the poverty line," notes another researcher, "increases in income have surprisingly little relation to personal happiness." Studies have shown that even those who have won a lottery haven't overall become significantly happier.

Andrew Carnegie and J. Paul Getty

Born in 1835 in Scotland, Andrew Carnegie came to the United States when he was thirteen. As an avid reader, he became largely self-educated. After working on a series of railroad jobs, he entered and subsequently revolutionized the steel industry. By 1889, he owned Carnegie Steel Corporation, the largest of its kind in the world. His new strategy helped him become the dominant force in the industry and an exceedingly wealthy man. It also made him known as one of America's "builders," as his business helped to fuel the economy and shape the nation into what it is today.

In 1901, at the age of 65, Carnegie made a dramatic change in his life. He sold his business, which earned him more than $200 million, and decided to spend the rest of his days helping others. While he had begun his philanthropic work years earlier by building libraries and making donations, he now expanded his efforts. He donated a substantial sum to the New York Public Library so that it could open several branches. Devoted to learning, he established the Carnegie Institute of Technology in Pittsburgh, now the Carnegie-Mellon University. In 1905, he created the Carnegie Foundation for the Advancement of Teaching. Strongly interested in peace, he formed the Carnegie Endowment for International Peace in 1910. It is said that over 2,800 libraries were opened with his support.

Early in the 1900s, a reporter interviewed Andrew Carnegie, who was then still one of the richest men in the world. "I am not to be envied," Carnegie told him. "How can my wealth help me? I am sixty years old and cannot digest my food. I would give all my millions if I could have youth and health."

The reporter then added: "Mr. Carnegie suddenly turned, and in hushed voice and with bitterness and depth of feeling quite indescribable, said, 'If I could make Faust's bargain I would. I would gladly sell anything to have my life over again.'"

Another multimillionaire, oil magnate J. Paul Getty, later said in agreement: "I would give my entire fortune for one happy marriage. Money doesn't necessarily have any connection with happiness. Maybe with unhappiness."

Benefits of Giving

Rather than wealth accumulation being the source of happiness, studies have shown a clear link between generosity and well-being. While possessing money or material goods doesn't make us happy, giving them away actually does.

For example, when people received a sum of money, they felt better if they spent it on others or gave it away, rather than spending it on themselves. Also, those who practice volunteering or donate to charity tend to have better physical, psychological and mental health, and greater longevity. Specifically in one study, donors have been found to have lower blood pressure, even when controlling for factors like income, wealth, age and exercise, which suggests the giving itself is responsible.

Research also showed that money is more likely to bring happiness if given away or if spent on experiences, rather than material goods. Another study suggests that a conscious lifestyle of "strategic under-consumption" or thrift can also lead to well-being.

So if you want to enhance your feeling of wellness and contentment, ignore the "happiness means consumption" messages that we are bombarded with by the media. A lifestyle of generosity and under-consumption may not suit the needs of economists and politicians - but it will make us individually happier.

We can learn much from the wise words of the American Indian, Ohiyesa, speaking of his Sioux people: "It was our belief that the love of possessions is a weakness to be overcome. Its appeal is to the material part, and if allowed its way, it will in time disturb one's spiritual balance. Therefore, children must early learn the beauty of generosity. They are taught to give what they prize most, that they may taste the happiness of giving."

Important Keys

As we can see, even if a materially high standard of living is realised, the hopes for happiness may never materialize because physical possessions of and by themselves, no matter how abundant, do not bring happiness, and money cannot buy it. Many a rich person, who seemingly had it all, also may have had poor health, unhappy marriage, several divorces and remarriages, chronic depression, and in the end may have even taken their own life or died in another tragic manner.

If a high standard of living was the key to happiness, people in the developed countries would have to be much happier than those in the developing world. Instead however, youth from well-to-do homes often live meaningless lives, seek happiness in destructive activities like drugs and alcohol, get into situations of violence, and even commit suicide.

Rather than focusing on purely material pursuits, put some of your energies into doing good – serving others. Focus on being compassionate, kind and helpful. Wish others well, instead of being jealous of their possessions or successes. Thoughts are powerful energy that influence both those we direct them to and ourselves. If we wish people well by sending them thoughts of kindness, these thoughts will come back to us. The same will happen if we project thoughts of hate and envy – those energies too will return to us like a boomerang. This is the law of cause and effect, or what goes around comes around.

Aligning with principles of ethics, morality and kindness is still the way to a happier life in contrast to harbouring greed, jealousy and anger. Respecting others and building them up with words of encouragement and acceptance is far more conducive to a life of peace and contentment for both the giver and the recipient than tearing down with criticism, arguing and strife.

Even though in our post-modern era there is seemingly no right or wrong, the fact is that beyond misguided thinking, universal principles still hold true. Therefore honesty and integrity will in reality never go out of style and in the long run, be the best policy. Being kind and considerate to others, not just concerned about self-satisfaction, will bring feelings of joy and well-being. If you are both frugal and generous – frugal in conservation, spending, and not being wasteful, and generous in giving and sharing – you will be blessed. This is because according to the higher principles of the universe, to give is more blessed than to receive, and it is generally better to be kind than to be right at all costs.

In summary, realize that happiness doesn't come from a pursuit of wealth and material possessions. There are indeed higher principles that will cause us to have a life abundant in joy and satisfaction. These include loving relationships, giving and serving others, and a life of kindness and compassion. Jesus is quoted as saying: "It is more blessed to give than to receive." (Bible, Acts 20:35).

For another insightful article, see
https://www.hopechannel.com/au/read/affluenza-what-does-your-money-say-about-you

Chapter 10
Practice Gratitude

I believe that one of the most important keys to happiness and contentment in life is gratitude. It ultimately means being thankful for all that is happening in our lives with the hope that even the unpleasant circumstances which we may experience will in some ways turn out for good – even when it is not clear how that could possibly happen. It includes seeing the good in the bad, realizing that things could always be worse, and being grateful that they aren't. It also means remembering with compassion those who are far worse off than we are – there is always someone – and appreciating our own situation.

Non-Material Blessings

Even if money is scarce, be grateful that you have the basic needs provided, such as food on the table and roof over your head. Being grateful even for the small things in life puts us in a place where we become more and more aware of the intangibles – those things that money cannot buy, but which can be worth more than winning a lottery jackpot.

Consider such things as the love of family and friends, the scent and beauty of spring flowers coming to life after a cold, dead winter, the sunshine and gentle breeze on your face, the fluttering butterfly that just flew past. Focus on the stars above, rather than the mud below and thereby rise above the negativity that often surrounds us in all forms and shapes. You cannot help but feel better about your situation.

It is a fact that our world generally reflects our thoughts – if we view our surroundings as negative and frustrating, that is how they will appear. If on the other hand, we focus on the bright side of life, or even the specks of light in the darkness, our view will be more optimistic.

Matter of Perspective

I am aware that in some parts of our sad world, many are living in hellish situations – especially when viewed from the affluent Western perspective. Yet, they make the most of their circumstances and often are more content than those of us whose challenges are infinitesimally smaller in comparison.

Also history is filled with stories of people who had survived concentration camps and similarly horrible situations by focusing on higher realities, by seeing meaning in their suffering, by maintaining a strong hope that life would get better, and by learning rich lessons from their trials and tribulations. Many of these survivors have been able to later improve their world by showing and teaching others how to transcend adversity despite all odds.

As contradictory as it may seem, research results reveal that adversity can actually increase gratitude. For example, an Internet survey has shown that after the events of September 11, 2001, there was an immediate surge in feelings of thankfulness. Tough times can actually deepen gratefulness if we allow them to remind us not to take things for granted. This is because in good times, we tend to take for granted what we should be grateful for. By contrast, in times of uncertainty, we often realize that the people and circumstances we've come to take for granted are actually of immense value to us.

Robert Emmons, Ph.D., writes: "In the face of demoralization, gratitude has the power to energize. In the face of brokenness, gratitude has the power to heal. In the face of despair, gratitude has the power to bring hope. In other words, gratitude can help us cope with hard times." In good times and in tough times, gratitude turns out to be one of the most powerful choices you can make.

Thankfulness and gratitude are principles that resonate through the various spiritual traditions. These qualities place us into a higher frame of mind, higher state of consciousness, higher vibrational energy. Even if things are bad, being grateful for the good things in our lot, no matter how infinitesimal, will invariably make us feel better. So as the Christian song goes, count your blessings one by one – and you may be surprised at how many you can come up with.

Health Benefits of Gratitude

Studies show that besides putting us in a better frame of mind, gratitude provides powerful health benefits, including vitality and inner peace. It not only makes us *feel* better – it also makes us *get* better physically, emotionally and mentally. Grateful people experience fewer aches and pains, better sleep, and stronger mental clarity.

It has been documented that a grateful attitude leads to measurable effects on several body and brain systems, including:

- Mood neurotransmitters (serotonin, norepinephrine)
- Reproductive hormones (testosterone)
- Social bonding hormones (oxytocin)
- Cognitive and pleasure related neurotransmitters (dopamine)
- Inflammatory and immune systems (cytokines)
- Stress hormones (cortisol)
- Cardiac and EEG rhythms
- Blood pressure
- Blood sugar

Overall Improved Situations

Another study has shown that when people over a period of ten weeks focused on what they could be grateful for rather than what annoyed them, they reported more life satisfaction and fewer health complaints than those with a negative orientation. A daily practice of recording things to be grateful for led to increased gratitude over time, as well as greater goodwill towards others. This manifested in giving more emotional support or helping others with their personal problems.

With a habitual focus on being grateful, changes occur in the brain which in turn lead to behaviour modification. As a result, grateful people tend to take better care of themselves and to engage in more protective health behaviours, like regular exercise and a healthy diet. They also tend to have lower levels of stress. This in turn is linked to increased immune function and to decreased rates of cancer and heart disease. The principle seems to be that grateful people take better care of what they appreciate – which extends to the body and other people.

Not only does saying "thank you" constitute good manners, but appreciating people can also win new friends and help build ongoing relationships. Grateful people also tend to be more sensitive and have greater empathy toward others, as well as a decreased desire to seek revenge.

Putting Gratitude to Work

To increase your GI ("Gratitude Quotient"), here are some simple things you can do:

1. *Say Grace:* Anytime you sit down to a meal with loved ones, or even by yourself, pause to give thanks for the food and other things in your life.

2. *Keep a daily gratitude journal:* Record what good things the day has brought and give thanks.

3. *Express gratefulness to those around you:* Tell a spouse, partner or friend every day what you appreciate about them.

4. *Remember mortality*: You never know how long you, or anyone close to you, will remain alive. Treat your loved ones as if this could be the last time you'll see them.

To sum up, gratefulness is a powerful attitude that will not only change your perspective and enable you to see a negative situation in a more positive light. It is also health promoting, modifies your overall behaviour, and contributes to building positive relationships.

For more information, see
http://foodrevolution.org/blog/thanksgiving/

Chapter 11
Possibility of a Higher Power

Sometimes we may feel like no one cares, no one loves us, nothing is going right, life is not fair, we aren't coping. And in the here and now, under the burdens many are facing, it may well seem that way. However, if you feel down and desperate, lost and lonely, or fearful and overwhelmed by your life's circumstances, consider that there may be a Higher Reality beyond the present physical experience that could help you improve your existence.

Consider the Existence of a Higher Reality

Many who have hit the rock bottom of their lives through addictions, business failures, relationship failures and heartbreak, terminal illness, or other hellish situations cried out in their despair to "God" for help. This was a last resort, just in case, plea when things can't get any worse and nothing can be lost – even if they weren't sure such a Being existed or was capable of hearing, much less helping.

And, lo and behold, miracles started happening. The highly successful Alcoholics Anonymous (AA) movement began on this principle, and since that time, many other programs have been built on the same foundation. Namely, there are certain aspects of our lives that we are unable to successfully handle ourselves and for which we need outside help. This is what has made the various "Anonymous" programs effective and successful – people in trouble appealing to a Higher Power as they understand it.

A Loving Helper

So if you are able to, accept and honour a Higher Reality as you understand it (God, Ultimate Cause, Ground of Being, the Universe, etc.). Consider that this Being / Reality is friendly and loving, not angry, judging, condemning and punishing as "He" may be often portrayed. Rather He/She is very willing to help us if we ask.

We are often "punished", or bad things happen to us, as a result of our own unwise choices or unskilful actions, or bad choices and actions of others. There is a very complex interaction of causes and effects that we are all subject to and potentially at the mercy of.

Yet if we raise our consciousness to a higher level, consider that what we experience with our physical senses is not all there is, and elevate our lifestyle from a level of just self-interest and personal gratification to a level of serving others, we'll receive help from unexpected sources. Generosity towards others will come back to us.

Looking for help beyond ourselves and believing that it will come will be rewarded. The universal principle of manifestation works more along the lines of "I'll see it when I believe it" than the other way around.

Overall, we live in a friendly universe based on the principle of love. Just look around and appreciate the beauty of flowers and animals, the provision of food and water from the nature around us, the sun being just the right distance from our little planet to give us climates and temperatures suitable for human life, and so much more. Of course, we can't deny the reality of suffering, but this is largely the result of causes and effects, of broken laws, of us or others abusing their free will.

The God understood by mystics and the various religions is indeed a Helper, Provider and Benefactor. This is true for all, but especially for those who honour and serve Him, and live in harmony with His laws meant to bring about human well-being.

Try asking for help in prayer. While our prayers may not be answered immediately, and/or exactly in the manner that we would like them to be, many people have experienced powerful answers and deliverances when they had prayed. Why go it alone, struggling with your limited human resources, when you can draw on the Power of the universe?

EPILOGUE

Chapter 12
Concluding Thoughts

Having finished this book is like coming to an end of a journey. It wasn't a long trip, but hopefully a memorable one with good lessons learned along the way.

We have taken a narrow path rather than the broad highway that many travel on. It has been uphill in parts. Effort and discipline were required to make it to the top and enjoy the view. In the process of climbing, some baggage had to be left behind. Several ups and downs were experienced. Failures and setbacks became stepping stones to successes as lessons were learned from them. New insights were gained into what makes us tick, how our thoughts and feelings powerfully influence our actions, what is really important, and how we can receive help from outside of us if we desire it.

On this trail, there are other peaks yet to be reached. But you have learned discipline, shed some weight, and are much fitter now, so the further climb will be easier. Continuing to apply the principles in the book (and other principles you'll learn along the path of life), will bring you to new views from the peaks yet ahead and new insights how to make your life even more abundant, satisfying and joyful.

So onward and upward ...

Different Concept of Success

Ralph Waldo Emerson gives an unconventional "definition" of success, but one worth considering. In his view, success is:

To laugh often and much;

To win the respect of intelligent people and the affection of children;

To earn the appreciation of honest critics and endure the betrayal of false friends;

To appreciate beauty, to find the best in others;

To leave the world a bit better, whether by a healthy child, a garden patch, or a redeemed social condition;

To know even one life has breathed easier because you have lived.

This is to have succeeded.

Interestingly, nothing is mentioned about money or possessions. There is nothing wrong with having wealth and material goods, but happiness and success don't depend on them. Neither can money buy peace, happiness and contentment.

The Bible, which even in our materialistic world is still respected by many as a valuable spiritual guide, says, quoting Jesus: "It is more blessed to give than to receive." Another Bible writer requested of God: "Give me neither poverty nor riches. Let me devour the food prescribed for me, that I may not become satisfied and I actually deny you and say: 'Who is Jehovah?' and that I may not come to poverty and I actually steal and assail the name of my God." (Proverbs 30:8-9).

King Solomon of ancient Israel, considered among the wisest humans of his time, commented: "I became greater and increased more than anyone that happened to be before me in Jerusalem." Yet, he concluded: "Everything was vanity and a striving after wind." Solomon also stated: "The blessing of Jehovah – that is what makes rich, and he adds no pain with it." (Ecclesiastes 2:9-11; 5:12, 13; Proverbs 10:22).

So there are higher principles, sometimes contrary to the common thinking, that come into play. Principles of love, kindness, giving and service – in short, consideration for the welfare of others as opposed to just self-gratification. Practicing these higher principles is what leads to well-being and happiness.

By way of review, let's briefly retrace the milestones encountered on our journey together.

Narrow Uphill Path

We have followed a road that not many in our western societies believe in taking nowadays. In a world where waiting is not in vogue, this is definitely the path less travelled, to borrow a line from Robert

Frost's famous poem. This is the path of delayed gratification – delayed until there is money on hand to acquire what we want. It is also a path of discipline – living within our means, rather than indiscriminate spending on whim and impulse.

A certain degree of sacrifice may be needed on this path – some belt tightening in order to get out of unnecessary debt, and to learn to live on less than previously. This, however, will all be worth it in the long run – when we get to the top of the hill. We'll have peace in not owing anyone more than is absolutely necessary, and in knowing that we have enough to meet our needs even if a major and unforeseen setback occurs. And, as time goes on, with proper money management including responsible saving, we'll be able to have many of our wants and desires as well. And at that time, having saved and waited, we'll be able to really appreciate these things.

As we practice continued financial discernment and discipline, save on credit card interest, as well as look after what we have to make it last longer, our resources, even if they are meager, will go a lot further.

Purposeful Climb

By taking a personal inventory of our life and seeing what we are good at, our climb can gain a purpose and focus. We can decide to use our gifts and talents to serve others – rather than just for selfish gain. This will in turn give us feelings of joy and satisfaction.

Besides finding out what we enjoy and can do well, it is important to take a look at our thinking. This is because thoughts are powerful energy which will influence our actions for better or worse. Remember that you can succeed if you really believe that you can. It may require a lot of determination, sacrifice, discipline, effort, and time, as well as learning all you can beforehand and as you go. However, if you persevere despite obstacles and setbacks, success is possible – the mountain peak can be reached. And the satisfaction of that, if the right goal has been pursued, will be well worth all the hard work and "blood, sweat and tears" along the way.

Help Alongside

Uphill climbing on a narrow trail can be challenging – especially with few others coming beside us on this road less travelled. Feeling tired, discouraged, lonely, and overwhelmed, as well as questioning if it is all worth it, can tempt us to give up and quit. However, if you keep your goal in mind and visualize the reward at the top, if you can be grateful for all parts of the journey – looking for the positive even in the negative, and if you can allow for the

Concluding Thoughts

possibility of the existence of something beyond the immediately visible, you may get help.

I believe in a loving Being – God, or whatever name others may have for the concept of a higher and benevolent Power beyond us. I also believe, based on decades of experience, that this Being wants us to succeed – like a father/mother wants their children to succeed. He / She desires for us to come with love and respect and ask for help in times of need, which He / She promises to provide.

Why not try this – you can't lose anything, you can only gain.

APPENDICES

Appendix 1
Living on a Budget

"Money makes the world go round", and all of us are certainly a part of that world. Since "money doesn't grow on trees", wise money management – planning how to use our money – makes sense. It doesn't mean cutting out all the fun from life or going without things we'd like. Budgeting actually makes money go further. Here are six tips that will ensure that you will have enough for your necessities, and in time, even your desires and dreams.

Income: Add up your total money received for a month or fortnight from all sources.

Outgo: Make a list of all your expenses for the same period of time as your income.

Balancing: Compare your income and outgo, and if your expenses exceed your income, make needed adjustments.

Checking: Keep track of where your money goes. For each pay period, record how much was spent for what.

Saving: Set aside a part of your income each month for the unexpected or for something special that you wish to purchase when you can afford it.

Investing: Put the money set aside for savings in the bank to avoid impulse spending.

At first, managing money this way may seem unnatural or even impossible. But don't give up – it will be well worth it. And finally, the better you learn to manage your money, the more money you'll have to manage!

Appendix 2
Income/Expense Analysis

It is important to know where our money goes to ensure that we are not overspending. Below are two simple tables for the purpose of illustrating how to keep track of income and outgo and how to avoid unnecessary debt.

Income Analysis

Bill receives a fixed salary every fortnight, while Jan works in a restaurant and her pay varies each pay period as a part of it comes in tips. The figures are just by way of example and for easy maths.

Month	Bill's pay	Jan's pay	Bank Interest	Total
Jan 1-15	520	250+ 100	0	870
Jan 16-31	520	250 + 67	20	857
Feb 1-15	520	250 + 55	0	825
Feb 16-28	520	250+ 120	18	908
Mar 1-15	520	250 + 88	0	858
Mar 16-31	520	250 + 76	15	861
Two-week average	**520**	**334**	**9**	**863**

Expense Analysis

In the following example, again actual numbers are not important and will vary from household to household and location to location. All we are doing is illustrating the principles.

Month	Food	Utilities	Rent	Misc.	Total
Jan 1-15	345	337	0	123	805
Jan 16-31	412	0	625	77	1114
Feb 1-15	320	350	0	98	768
Feb 16-28	355	0	625	131	1111
March 1-15	400	341	0	69	810
Mar 16-31	425	0	625	85	1135
Two-week average	**376**	**171**	**313**	**97**	**957**

Note that upon comparing the income totals with the expense totals, the expenses exceed the income by about 10%. In such a case, adjustments should be made so as not to keep overspending and increasing credit card debt – which, to add insult to injury, accrues high interest.

Appendix 3
The Power of Thought

As mentioned in Chapter 6, our thoughts and perceptions influence how we feel about a situation. For example, a negative situation can change simply by changing our perspective about it and vice versa.

Here are some interesting quotes on the subject of thinking from various authors and traditions:

- The world is a reflection of your thoughts. Change your thoughts, change your life. (Notsalmon.com)

- Change *I can't* into *I can* and pretty soon you will be saying *I did*. (Unknown author)

- Positive thoughts are more powerful than negative ones and you can choose which you pay attention to. (Paul Foreman, www.mindmapinspiration.com)

- A man is but a product of his thoughts. What he thinks, he becomes. (Gandhi)

- Life is the movie you see through your own, unique eyes. It makes little difference what's happening out there. It's how you take it that counts. (Denis Waitley, *The Winner's Edge*)

- Experience is determined by yourself – not the circumstances of your life. (Gita Bellin)

- To find yourself, think for yourself. (Socrates)

- Dwell not on the past. Use it to illustrate a point, then leave it behind. Nothing really matters except what you do now in this instant of time. From this moment onward you can be an entirely different person, filled with love and understanding, ready with an outstretched hand, uplifted and positive in every thought and deed. (Eileen Caddy, *God Spoke to Me*)

- We are what we think. All that we are arises with our thoughts. With our thoughts we make the world. Speak or act with a pure mind and happiness will follow you as your shadow, unshakeable. (*The Dhammapada*)

- Thoughts are things; they have tremendous power. Thoughts of doubt and fear are pathways to failure. When you conquer negative attitudes of doubt and fear, you conquer failure. Thoughts crystallize into habit and habit solidifies into circumstances. (Brian Adams, *How to Succeed*)

- You are given the gifts of the gods; you create your reality according to your beliefs. Yours is the creative energy that makes your world. There are no limitations to the self except those you believe in. (Jane Roberts, *The Nature of Personal Reality*)

- Be at peace and see a clear pattern and plan running through all your lives. Nothing is by chance. (Eileen Caddy, *Footprints on the Path*)

- What we are today comes from our thoughts of yesterday, and our present thoughts build our life of tomorrow: our life is the creation of our mind. (The Buddha)

- Everything I do and say with anyone makes a difference. (Gita Bellin)

- Thoughts are like boomerangs. (Eileen Caddy, *The Dawn of Change*)

- There is little sense in attempting to change external conditions, you must first change inner beliefs, then outer conditions will change accordingly. (Brian Adams, *How to Succeed*)

- Success depends on where intention is. (Gita Bellin)

- You should always be aware that your head creates your world. (Ken Keyes, Jr., *Handbook to Higher Consciousness*)

- Until you can understand that nothing can happen to you, nothing can ever come to you or be kept from you, except in accord with your state of consciousness, you do not have the key to life. (Paul Twitchell)

- A loving person lives in a loving world. A hostile person lives in a hostile world. Everyone you meet is your mirror. (Ken Keyes, Jr., *Handbook to Higher Consciousness*)

- Each player must accept the cards life deals him or her. But once they are in hand, he or she alone must decide how to play the cards in order to win the game. (Voltaire)

- Life has a bright side and a dark side, for the world of relativity is composed of light and shadows. If you permit your thoughts to dwell on evil, you yourself will become ugly. Look only for the good in everything, that you absorb the quality of beauty. (Paramahansa Yogananda, *Sayings of Paramahansa Yogananda*)

- A man must elevate himself by his own mind, not degrade himself. The mind is the friend of the conditioned soul, and his enemy as well. (*Bhagavad-Gita*, VI:5)

Appendix 4
Visualization and Affirmations

The following tips were adopted from Jack Canfield's book, *The Success Principles*.

Often we act like driving a car with the hand brake on – maintaining a psychological brake of negative images and wrong beliefs. This keeps us comfortable – but limited. The key is to get out of our comfort zone by creating powerful internal *images* of what we want, and using positive *affirmations* or self-talk that reflect our goals fulfilled. Over time, this will lead to changing our behaviour and achieving our goals.

Imagination and visualization are very powerful tools. The brain sees no difference between visualizing something and actually doing it. One hour of visualization may be worth several hours of physical effort.

Visualization activates the creative powers of the subconscious mind; focuses the brain to notice relevant available resources; and attracts to us the people, resources and opportunities needed for achieving our goal. The conflict created in the subconscious between the present and visualized reality is resolved by opening doors for bringing about the new reality. This occurs through processes such as generating helpful thoughts and ideas, creating motivation to do new things, and empowering us to step out of our comfort zone and take more risks.

Visualize what you want to achieve with colours, sounds and feelings. For a stronger effect, make a goal notebook or vision board with photos and/or illustrations. To create effective affirmations, put your vision into a present-tense, first-person statement as though it was already reality. For example, "I am enjoying being … ."

Repeat and vividly visualize your affirmation one to three times a day, starting in the morning. You can also post it on cards around the house, record and listen to it, repeat and visualize it while you wait – the opportunities are endless. Daily meditation followed by affirming and visualizing your goal can be a powerful tool for reprogramming your mind and facilitating the achievement of your goals.

About the Author

Eva Peck has an international and Christian background. Having lived and worked in Australia, the United States, Europe, Asia, and the Middle East, including teaching English as a foreign language, she has experienced a range of cultures, customs, and environments. She now draws on those experiences in her writing.

Eva has a Bachelor's degree in Biological Sciences, a post-graduate Diploma in Education, and a Master's degree in Theology. Besides working for schools and other institutions, she also has small business experience, as well as experience in financial management on which she is drawing in this book.

Eva lives in Brisbane, Australia, with her husband, Alex.

About Pathway Publishing

Pathway Publishing is dedicated to sharing truth and beauty by publishing books and producing websites that present what is true to life and reality, as well as what is lovely and inspirational. The goal is to not only provide sound information, but also to uplift the human spirit.

Pathway Publishing has a vision of enriching the life of readers here and now, as well as helping them on their path of enlightenment and spiritual transformation. The wisdom and experience of spiritual teachers, thinkers, and visionary writers from various backgrounds and faith traditions are recognized and valued.

Books produced by Pathway Publishing broadly fall into two categories – spirituality and the arts – and include:

- *Divine Reflections in Times and Seasons*, Eva Peck
- *Divine Reflections in Natural Phenomena*, Eva Peck
- *Divine Reflections in Living Things*, Eva Peck
- *Divine Insights from Human Life,* Eva Peck
- *Pathway to Life - Through the Holy Scriptures,* Eva and Alexander Peck
- *Journey to the Divine Within – Through Silence, Stillness and Simplicity,* Alexander and Eva Peck
- *Jesus' Gospel of God's Love*, Eva Peck

- *Abundant Living on Small Income*, Eva Peck
- *The Greatest Love*, Eva Peck
- *Salvation*, Eva Peck
- *Problem of Evil*, Eva Peck
- *Answers to Prayer*, Eva Peck
- *The Bible as a Guide to Life*, Eva Peck
- *Life After Death*, Eva Peck
- *Jesus Christ – A New Look at His Identity and Mission*, Eva Peck and Michael Nedbal
- *Fulfillments of Old Testament Types*, Eva Peck

- *Artistic Inspirations - Paintings of Jindrich Degen* arranged by Eva and Alexander Peck
- *Colour and Contrast – Artwork of Jindrich Degen* arranged by Eva and Alexander Peck
- *Faces and Forms Across Time – Artwork of Jindrich Degen*, arranged by Eva and Alexander Peck
- *Variations – Art Exhibition of Jindrich Degen*, arranged by Eva and Alex Peck
- *Floral and Nature Art – Photography of Jindrich Degen*, arranged by Eva and Alexander Peck
- *Nature's Beauty – Art Photography of Jindrich Degen*, arranged by Eva and Alex Peck

- *Volné verše,* Jindrich Degen (Czech poetry)

- *Verše pro dnešní dobu,* Jindrich Degen (Czech poetry)
- *Pardál za úplňku a jiné povídky,* Eva Vaníčková (Czech stories set mostly in Indonesia)

http://www.pathway-publishing.org/

Pathway Publishing
Seeking truth and beauty

Pathway Publishing
Seeking truth and beauty

www.ingramcontent.com/pod-product-compliance
Lightning Source LLC
Chambersburg PA
CBHW021130300426
44113CB00006B/365